The Stor[y]

Large crowds gathered on the morning of Saturaay 14th September 1805, as Horatio Nelson headed through the streets of Portsmouth to join his ship HMS Victory which was waiting for him in the Solent. These would be the last steps that Nelson took on dry land, as 37 days later he was killed aboard his ship at the Battle of Trafalgar by a French sniper.

On the morning of his departure, Nelson left a valuable diamond necklace that he had bought for his beloved Lady Hamilton in a chest in one of Portsmouth's many taverns for safekeeping. The following day, the tavern was broken into, and the necklace was stolen.

Solve the mystery by eliminating clues to find the name, age, and occupation of the thief, as well as the name of the tavern, and the evidence left at the scene.

The diamond necklace story is fictional, but all historical facts included in the treasure hunt are true

HOW TO PLAY

1
Follow the Maps
to find the location
of your clue

2
Solve the Clue to eliminate one
option from the list on page 1
(Extra help is on the back page)

3
At each stop you will
Unravel more of
the legendary tale.

4
At the end of your adventure your last
remaining items on Page 1 will
Reveal the final Secrets of the Mystery

IMPORTANT INFORMATION

1 On rare occasions, clues may be temporarily covered or permanently removed. In this instance we ask you to use the extra clues at the back o the book, and if possible, please report this to us.
It is recommended that you do the activity within 3 months of purchase, to reduce this risk.

2 Take care! You are responsible for yourself and your group. Be careful crossing roads, make sure to respect old monuments and private property, and if you are drinking alcohol please drink responsibly.

3 Any food & drink discounts available in this booklet are at the discretion of the stated premises, and may be subject to change or cancellation.

Starting point:

The starting point for the treasure hunt is at **the statue of Nelson in Grand Parade**, Old Portsmouth., **PO1 2NF.** (near the Royal Garrison Church)

Once you have arrived at the start point you can begin the hunt!

By bus: Take public transport to **The Hard Interchange** and then walk 7-10 mins to the start point following the route map below.

By train: Take the train to **Portsmouth Harbour** station and then walk 7-10 mins to the start point following the route map below.

By car: Many parking spaces are available at **Gunwharf Quays.**

Alternatively there is a nearer but much smaller carpark at the **Bridge Tavern.** (see map)

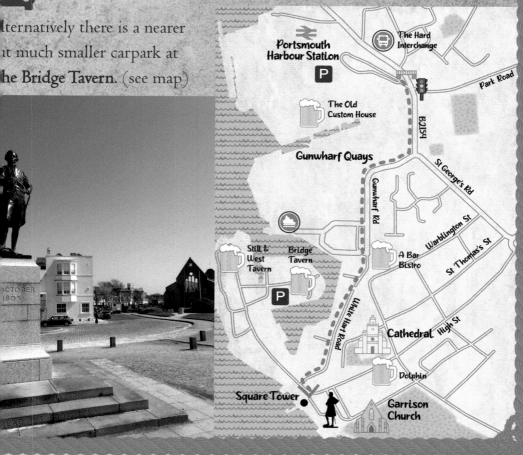

Clue I

 The location of your first clue can be seen from Nelson's statue.

'Your first clue is at a *place of God*, where the feet of Kings and Queens once trod.

The two sides of the outer gate, form a strong dark metal shape.'

Eliminate a **tavern** from your list

(Extra help on page 41 if you get stuck)

5

Did you know?

The Royal Garrison Church was once known as 'Domus Dei' (House of God) and it was here on 9th January 1450 that the Bishop of Chichester Adam Moleyns was murdered by an angry mob in a dispute over the payment of local troops. The sitting Pope was so outraged by the murder that the whole island of Portsmouth was excommunicated from the Catholic Church for 58 years.

The church was also the site for the royal wedding between Charles II and Catherine of Braganza in 1662.

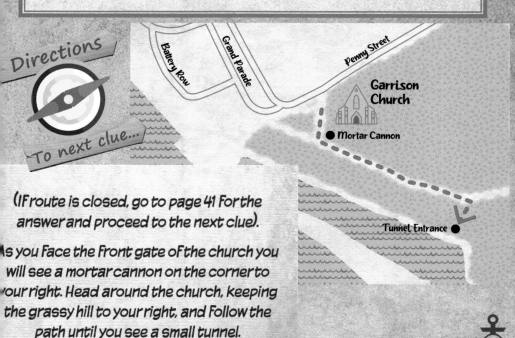

Directions

To next clue...

(If route is closed, go to page 41 for the answer and proceed to the next clue).

As you face the front gate of the church you will see a mortar cannon on the corner to your right. Head around the church, keeping the grassy hill to your right, and follow the path until you see a small tunnel.

Clue 2

The tunnel in front of you forms part of the defensive structure known as 'The Long Curtain' which was designed by Dutch engineer Sir Bernard de Gomme in the 1670s. The tunnel is also the place where Horatio Nelson took his final steps on dry land, before leaving to fight in the battle of Trafalgar in 1805.

Eliminate an **<u>occupation</u>** associated with the name of the defensive structure

(For this clue, you don't need to find anything at the location)

Did you know?

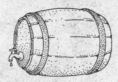

After Nelson's death his body was brought back to England preserved in a barrel of brandy (not rum as is commonly thought). Legend has it that by the time the barrel was opened, all of the liquor had been secretly drunk by the sailors on board. Herein lies the origin of a navy expression "tapping the Admiral" which is used to describe the act of secretly drinking alcohol.

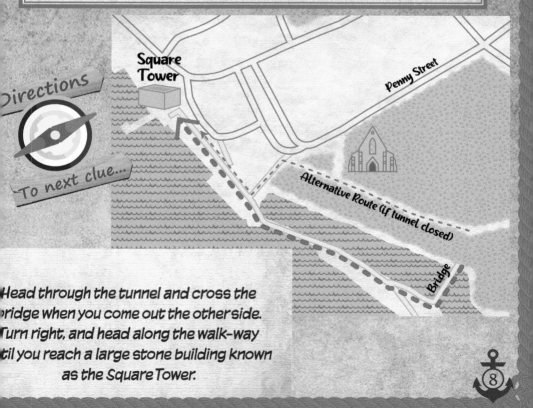

Square Tower

Penny Street

Directions

To next clue...

Alternative Route (if tunnel closed)

Bridge

Head through the tunnel and cross the bridge when you come out the other side. Turn right, and head along the walk-way til you reach a large stone building known as the Square Tower.

F/6

H

A/I

Z

S

G/7

In 1823 the Admiralty added a semaphore tower to the roof of the Square Tower to enable them to send orders from London to the ships stationed in the Solent. Convert Nelson's pose in the painting to the most similar semaphore flag to **eliminate a <u>suspect</u>**.

(You don't need to find anything at the location to solve this clue)

Did you know?

In the 16th century the Square Tower changed use from the Governor's residence, to a gunpowder store capable of holding over 1,200 barrels. During the English Civil War the Royalist Governor of Portsmouth George Goring surrendered while the city was under siege, but threatened to blow up the Square Tower unless he was allowed to flee to the Netherlands. When sailing out of the city he threw the keys to the city overboard. Miraculously these keys were found while dredging Portsmouth Harbour in the 19th century, and were put on display in Southsea Castle.

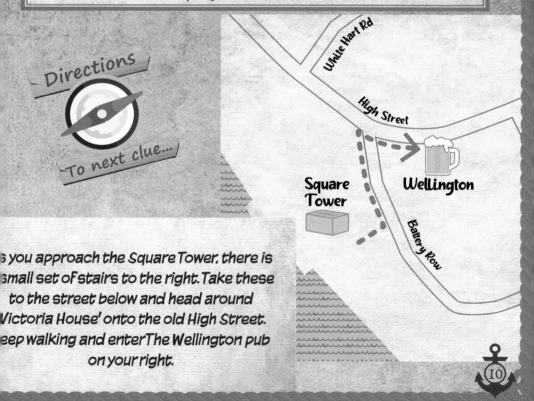

Directions

To next clue...

White Hart Rd

High Street

Square Tower

Wellington

Battery Row

s you approach the Square Tower, there is small set of stairs to the right. Take these to the street below and head around Victoria House' onto the old High Street. eep walking and enter The Wellington pub on your right.

Did you know?

PUB STOP 1

The Wellington

The pub is named after Arthur Wellesley, the 1st Duke of Wellington and the famous hero of the Battle of Waterloo.

Earlier you found your first clue at the Royal Garrison church. In 1559 a large mansion was built onto the side of that church, which was used as the residence for the Governor of Portsmouth. In 1814 that mansion was the venue for a star-studded party to celebrate the defeat of Napoleon at the Battle of Leipzig. Notable guests included the Prince Regent, the Emperor of Russia, and the man himself, the Duke of Wellington. Large crowds gathered to catch a glimpse of the hero in the streets around this pub, with drunken celebrations lasting several days.

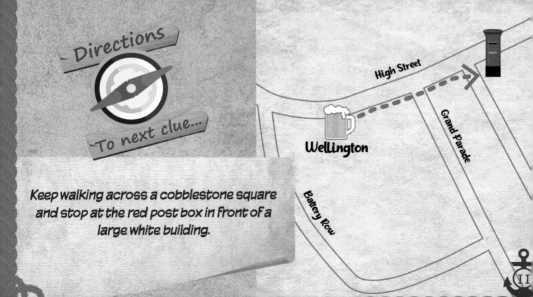

Directions

To next clue...

Keep walking across a cobblestone square and stop at the red post box in front of a large white building.

High Street

Wellington

Grand Parade

Battery Row

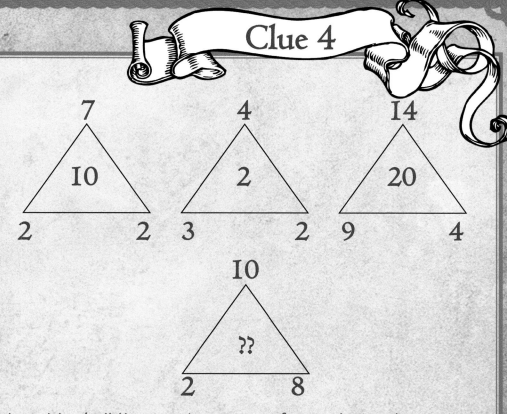

The white building on the corner of Grand Parade was once Grant & Madison's Union Bank, which was taken over by Lloyds in 1903. Although now a private house, the original vaults still exist in the basement.

Use the numbers on the outside of the triangles to make the number in the centre. The first 3 triangles all use the same equation. Work out this equation, and then use it to calculate the number in the final triangle. You can use addition, subtraction, or multiplication (+, −, ×).

Eliminate an _age_

Did you know?

If you look at the Square Tower from here, you will see a bust of Charles I looking down the old High Street. This street is in fact the terminal point of the A3 which in the 18th century served a direct 8.5-hour horse and coach route to the city of London. Known as 'the Sailors Highway', this treacherous route was synonymous with highwaymen looking to rob wealthy officers and noblemen.

Directions

To next clue...

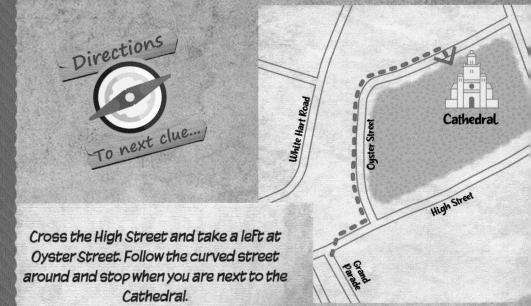

Cross the High Street and take a left at Oyster Street. Follow the curved street around and stop when you are next to the Cathedral.

Find this skull on the outside of the Cathedral.

Facing death, two heads are better than one.

Eliminate an **age** from your list

Did you know?

You are currently in St Thomas's Street, which featured in Charles Dickens' third novel Nicholas Nickleby. It is known that Dickens returned to Portsmouth (his birth city) to research the novel. Nickleby stayed in the house of 'Mr Crummles' (house number unknown) while he worked in the High Street.

Directions

To next clue...

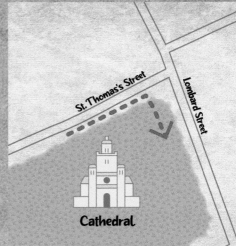

St. Thomas's Street

Lombard Street

Cathedral

High Street

Continue along St. Thomas's Street and enter the Cathedral Garden on the corner.

For your next clue you need to
enter the Cathedral garden.

In the small Cathedral garden, the next clue you shall *meet.*
Five *familiar* people, lie together at your feet.

Eliminate an **occupation** from your list. **If you can't enter the garden turn to page 41 for an extra clue.**

Did you know?

At the very top of the Cathedral is a weathervane known as the 'Golden Barque'. Historically when this was taken down for cleaning, superstitious local residents would put their young children's feet in this boat, believing that this act would prevent them from ever drowning at sea.

Directions

To next clue...

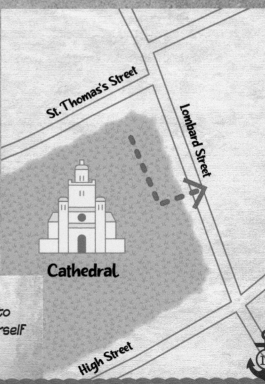

St. Thomas's Street

Lombard Street

Cathedral

High Street

Exit the Garden at the opposite end to which you entered. You will now find yourself on Lombard Street

Clue 7

4.57   8.45   12.25

In this street lives a <u>big and precious cat</u>,
you won't find it sitting on a door mat.
Find its position, looking out at you,
And from its shape, you can solve this clue.

*Keeping the Cathedral garden on your left hand side,
use the front half of the animal as the small clock hand
and the back half of the animal as the big clock hand to
<u>eliminate a time from your list</u>.*

Did you know?

This street was once called 'Golden Lion Lane', and the house holding the clue was once a pub called the 'Golden Lion'.

An essential piece of kit aboard a Royal Navy ship was the Cat o' Nine Tails which was an 80cm long leather whip used to publicly flog unruly sailors on deck. From this practice we get the expressions 'enough room to swing a cat', and 'to let the cat out of the bag'.

Directions

To next clue...

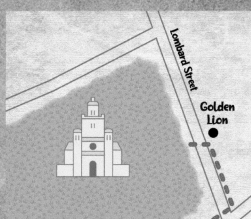

As you face the golden lion, turn right and walk towards the High Street. Across the road you will see a pub called The Dolphin.

Your next clue is inside the Dolphin pub.
(If you can't enter, go to P41 for the answer)

Did you know?

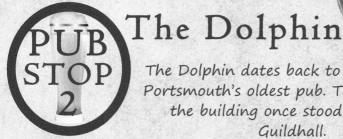

PUB STOP 2

The Dolphin

The Dolphin dates back to 1716 and is Portsmouth's oldest pub. To the right of the building once stood the city's Guildhall.

One of the perks of working in a Royal Navy dockyard was the right to take home a daily allowance of offcuts of timber; much of which was sold as building material for the city's pubs such as this one. This practice became extremely costly to the taxpayer, so in 1757 the Navy ordered that only wood that could be carried under the arm (not over the shoulder) could be taken. This is one theory for the origin of the phrase 'chip on his shoulder'.

Clue 8

'In Portsmouth Nelson *made his name*, this place was once his patch.
Inside the Dolphin hangs the clue, you need to start from *scratch*.'

Find the item Nelson used to make his name and eliminate it from your <u>list of evidence</u>. If you can't enter the pub go to page 41 for an extra clue.

As you leave the Dolpin, turn right and continue along the Hight Street for around 3 minutes until you reach an old green building which was the location for the assassination of the Duke of Buckingham (plaque outside).

Directions

To next clue...

Green Hous

...s's Street

Peacock Lane

Lombard Street

High Street

Farthing Lane

The Dolphin

Clue 9

Spot your next clue when John Felton was *hounded*.

Eliminate a <u>time</u> from your list.

Take a photo

Tag on social media: @mysteryguides

For a chance to win a prize!!

PHOTO STOP!

Did you know?

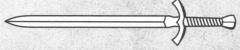

The Duke of Buckingham was the lover of James I, and Lord Admiral for Charles I, but was despised by the people of England due to his incompetent military leadership and luxurious lifestyle. He was murdered in this house by John Felton, an army officer who had been wounded in an earlier military campaign. After being hanged in London, the body of Felton was displayed in Portsmouth as a warning to the local population who had largely celebrated the Duke's death. It was such a big event that 30 years later Samuel Pepys visited this place and wrote about it in his diary.

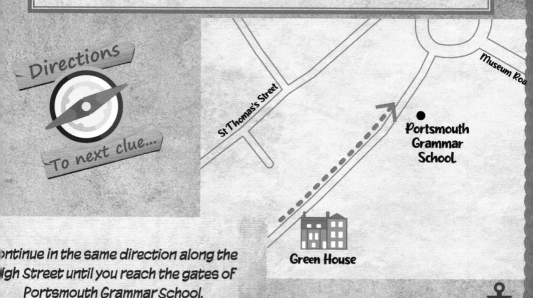

Directions

To next clue...

ontinue in the same direction along the
igh Street until you reach the gates of
Portsmouth Grammar School.

St Thomas's Street

Museum Roa

Portsmouth
Grammar
School

Green House

Clue 10

In order to relieve the local population from the behaviour of billeted troops, Cambridge Barracks was built in 1825 by converting a number of buildings (including military warehouses and a brewery) into the large complex you see in front of you today. This area later expanded by knocking down other key high street landmarks.

Look at the outside of the school

'Torn down in 1854,
Nicholas Nickleby would have used this floor.'

Eliminate an **occupation** from your list

Did you know?

In the famous novel, While living with Mr Crummles in St Thomas's Street, Nicholas Nickleby took a job as an actor in this theatre.

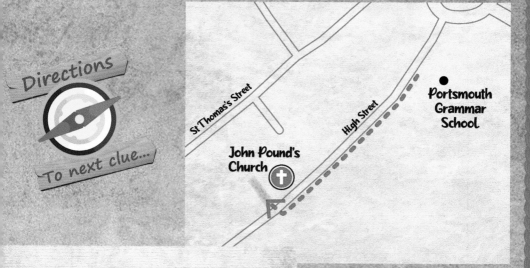

Directions

To next clue...

Cross the High Street and head back down the High Street in the direction of the Cathedral. On your right hand side you will see John Pounds Church (opposite the site of Buckingham's assassination).

Enter the Garden to the left of the Church.

Enter the John Pounds memorial garden

John Pounds was born in 1766 when Portsmouth was a rough and deprived city. High concentrations of troops and sailors, along with widespread
drinking and prostitution led to large numbers of orphans who had very little hope of a future. John Pounds devoted his life to helping children learn to read from his local cobblers shop after being disabled in a terrible accident while working in the dockyard aged just 15. This church was named in his honour.

'Find John himself with children sharing,
Eliminate an object that he is wearing.'

Eliminate an item of <u>evidence</u> from your list. **If you can't enter the garden then go to page 41 for an extra clue.**

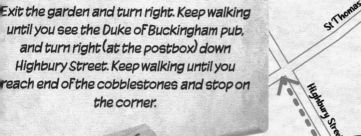

Exit the garden and turn right. Keep walking until you see the Duke of Buckingham pub, and turn right (at the postbox) down Highbury Street. Keep walking until you reach end of the cobblestones and stop on the corner.

Directions

To next clue...

St Thomas's Street

John Pound's Church

High Street

Highbury Street

The Duke of Buckingham

Peacock Lane

Clue 12

Search the corner of Highbury Street,
the answer lies beneath your feet.
The clue is *initially* hard to find,
curb thoughts of quitting from your mind.

Eliminate a **suspect** from your list

Did you know?

As you follow the directions below you will see a beautiful example of 17th century Dutch-style houses on the corner of Lombard Street (opposite the Cathedral). In the age before military barracks, during times of conflict soldiers were temporarily lodged in people's private houses in an unpopular practice known as 'billeting'. Under the reign of James II Portsmouth had the largest concentration of soldiers outside of London, bringing chaos to the city along with a huge rise in drunkenness, violence, and theft.

Directions

To next clue...

A Bar Bistro

Lombard Street

Highbury Street

St Thomas's Street

17th Century Houses

Leaving the cobblestones of Highbury Street behind you, turn left and head back towards the Cathedral until you get to Lombard Street. Turn right when you see the Dutch-style houses on the corner. Continue along Lombard Street and you will see A Bar Bistro on the corner.

Did you know?

A Bar Bistro

PUB STOP 3

In 1887 the 'A Bar' was known as 'The American Hotel'. Legend has it that it's name derives from the building's original use as a jail for convicts waiting to be deported to penal colonies in Virginia during the 18th century.

Clue 13

D	W	O
E	G	P
R	U	N

Find a 9-letter word in this grid. The nine letters form a continuous line passing through each square once without crossing itself. This word is associated with a **name of a tavern** that you should eliminate from your list.

As you leave the pub, take a left and walk through some bollards. Keep walking until you see a small alley on your right called 'Feltham Row'. Follow this all the way around - you will exit onto a main road with some brick arches on the other side. Stop within the large pedestrian area opposite the arches.

Directions

To next clue...

White Hart Rd

A Bar Bistro

Feltham Row

Broad Street

Did you know?

The archways in front of you were once part of a huge enclosed area known as 'Point Barracks' which were constructed in 1847. In order to make way for the barracks at least 8 notorious drinking dens were destroyed, including the famous 'Blue Anchor', 'Queen's Head', and 'Fortune of War'.

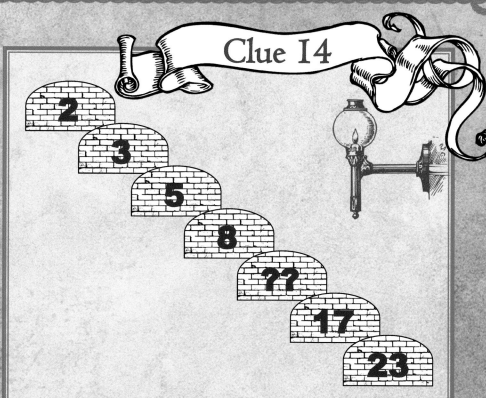

2

3

5

8

??

17

23

Solve the puzzle to find the missing number.

If it's an **odd** number eliminate <u>Moses Levy</u>.
If it's an **even** number eliminate <u>Frances Hogarth</u>.

Directions

To next clue...

Tower Street

Tower Alley

Capstan
Square

The Round
Tower

Broad Street

At the top of the old Point Barracks
(archway complex) you will see a red phone
box on the corner. Immediately after this on
the left is a small alleyway lined with
reclaimed boat timbers. Follow the alley to
the bottom and into a small area known as
Capstan Square which is in the shadow of
the Round Tower.

Did you know?

There was once a 'mighty chain of iron' that ran
from here across the entrance of the harbour that
could be raised in order to stop enemy ships from
entering. workmen excavating the harbour in 1930
found several of these links that were 3ft 9 inches in
length and thought to have originated from 1664. A
reproduction can be found on display in this square.

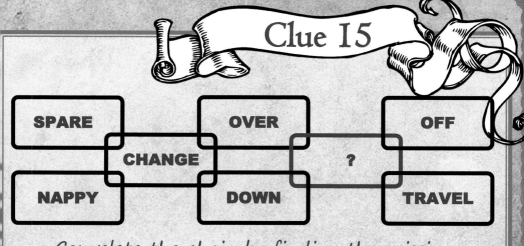

Clue 15

SPARE		OVER		OFF
	CHANGE		?	
NAPPY		DOWN		TRAVEL

Complete the chain by finding the missing word.

The word must follow 'over' and 'down' and precede 'off' and 'travel'.

Eliminate an <u>item</u> relating to that word.

Directions

To next clue...

Exit Capstan Square and immediately turn left into the small alley known as Tower Street. Your next clue is within this short stretch of alleyway.

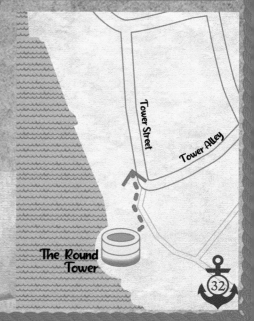

Tower Street

Tower Alley

The Round Tower

Clue 16

Your next clue can be found in this short stretch of alleyway.

'Outside a former tavern,
a date waits for you.
Find this black beauty,
To eliminate a clue.'

Eliminate a <u>time</u> from your list.

Did you know?

The young Prince William Henry who later became King William IV served time in the Royal Navy in his youth, and eventually became known as 'The Sailor King'. On one evening the Prince was drinking in a tavern in this alley and accidentally drank a local waterman's ale. On refusing to buy him another, a fight ensued and the Prince was badly beaten. The waterman later found out the identity of the man who he had beaten up, and was mortified when he was summoned to the Admiral's house. To his surprise the waterman was offered a good job in the Customs Service if he agreed to never speak of the fight again.

Directions
To next clue...

Spice Island

Broad Street

East Street

Former Seagull Tavern ●

West Street

Tower Street

Continue down Tower Street and take the first right into West Street. You will see the Former Seagull Tavern on your left. Take the first left to the end of Broad Street; you will notice the old tram lines in the middle of the road. When you get to the very end of the street you will see a seat area surrounded by a small brick wall. Enter this area and look back at the Spice Island Inn.

Did you know?

You are now in front of the popular pub, the 'Spice Island Inn', which was originally formed of several smaller independent taverns known by various names. At one time Spice Island itself (the area from here to the Square Tower) had almost 50 pubs, and had a widely known reputation for drunkenness, violence and prostitution. It was said that sailors 'earned their money like horses and spent it like asses'. Nowhere was this more true than on Spice Island.

Clue 17

<u>Face the front of the Spice Island Inn</u>

'Two Clues left you're almost there,
the evidence should stick.
Find the pub's former name,
painted high up on brick.'

Eliminate the name of the <u>tavern</u>

Follow the road round the Spice Island Inn
and you will find another famous
Portsmouth pub, 'The Still & West'.

Directions

To next clue...

Spice
Island

Broad Street

Bath Square

The Still
& West

The Still & West

Dating back to 1733, this pub was originally called the Still, named after the pipe from the Bosun's whistle that was used to summon deck-hands serving in the Royal Navy for dinner ('piping hot food') or to call them to sleep ('pipe down').

In 1882 the daughter of the East & West Country House Tavern (which was just around the corner), married the owner of the Still, and the names were combined.

Leave 'The Still & West' and turn right. Keep walking and stop outside a large white wooden building known as 'Quebec House' located in Bath Square.

Directions

To next clue...

The Still & West

Broad Street

Bath Square

Bathing Lane

Quebec House

Did you know?

This building was built in 1754 to serve as a saltwater bathing house, hence the name of the square. It later became the Quebec Hotel, named in honour of the famous capture of Quebec from the French in 1759.

In 1845 England's last ever fatal duel happened just over the water in Gosport between Captain James Seton and Lieutenant Henry Hawkey. Seton had danced with Hawkey's wife Isabella at a ball held in Southsea, which led to an altercation between the pair. The next day Seton challenged Hawkey to a duel, and pistols were purchased. Seton was shot in the abdomen, and taken back across the water to this very building where he died. In the resulting court case duelling was made illegal in England.

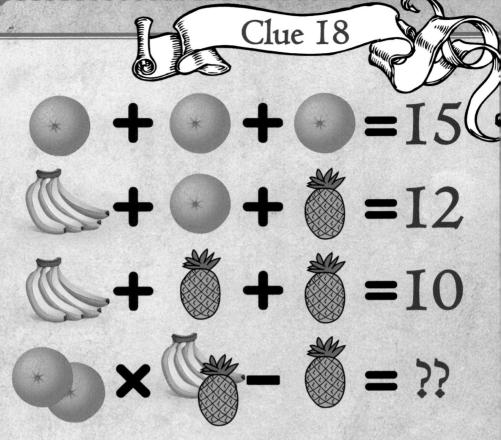

Bath Square was once a bustling market, selling all kinds of products that had been shipped into Portsmouth from far away places. Items for sale included tobacco, wine, and exotic fruits.

Solve the puzzle to **eliminate an age**. (when 2 fruits are placed together they should be added)

Congratulations!

You have finished all of the clues, and you should now have all of the information you need to solve the mystery.

First, we need to return to the scene of the crime.

The directions below will lead you to the last remaining pub on your list, which has a **famous painting on its outside**

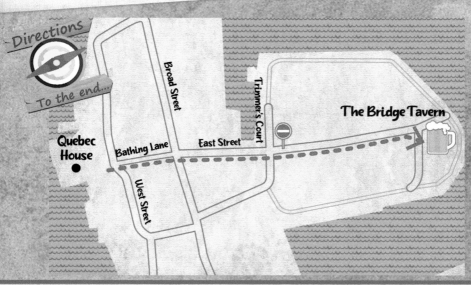

Directions

To the end...

Quebec House

Broad Street

Bathing Lane

West Street

Trimmer's Court

East Street

The Bridge Tavern

PUB STOP 5

The Bridge Tavern

The name of this pub derives from a swing bridge which was constructed on this site in 1842. The small tidal inlet of water next to the pub is known as 'The Camber', and is the original site of the town of Portsmouth, founded in 1180 by Jean De Gisors. In the 18th century The Camber was leased by the East India Company, who used it to import spices from the Caribbean, giving the area the name 'Spice Island'. Others say the name derives from the terrible stench of the area, as it was used as an open sewer and unloading point for pigs and cattle.

The painting on the outside of the pub is a copy of the original engraving you will see on the right, titled 'Portsmouth Point', made by the famous political cartoonist Thomas Rowlandson in 1811.

Look carefully at the engraving below, and by using your last remaining clues on page 1, you should be able to identify the guilty ◆ diamond thief! ◆

Find the suspect in the painting that matches the description of your remaining items:

SUSPECT   OCCUPATION   EVIDENCE

Extra Clues Page

ue 1: When the church gate is closed, the two sides form an iron heart.

ue 2: A draper makes curtains.

ue 3: The answer can be found in French number 7.

ue 4: Subtract the bottom left from the top and multiply by the bottom right.

ue 5: The skull faces a house with two heads outside. Eliminate the house

ue 6: One gravestone in the centre of the path has 5 people listed on it who belong to the same family. The surname is the clue. If you can't find the ...vestone, unscramble the anagram: c r b t e h u ...mber from your list of ages. (The youngest)

ue 7: Find a golden lion at house number 6. Its head is pointing just after 12.

ue 8: On the wall of the pub is a famous pane of glass that was the window of ...Star & Garter pub. Legend has it that Horatio Nelson himself carved his ...tials into the glass with a diamond ring that can still be seen today.

ue 9: On the side of the building is a plaque that tells you the original name ...the pub. translate this date to a time. (15:)

ue 10: On the side of the school you will see a plaque that describes a ...ilding, theatrically torn down in 1854. Eliminate an occupation.

ue 11: At the back of the garden is a replica of John Pounds' shoe shop. ...side stands the man himself who is wearing an object on his face.

ue 12: Look for initials on the kerb on the corner of Highbury Street. check ...ery Last stone!

ue 13: Start at the centre and go down and then right.

ue 14: Add the number in the arch to its position in the line.

ue 15: Hurry up! You are running out of this...

ue 16: A plaque on the wall of a former tavern will show you a year. translate ...s to a time. (16:)

ue 17: Above the name 'Spice Island Inn' you will see the pub's former ...me in faded writing (top left). Work on this together.

ue 18: A pineapple is worth 3.

41